Jettison the Junk

Introduction

Several years ago, I was faced with one of the hardest situations I had to bear. In a year, several events took place that I was not prepared to handle. As a result, I ended up with severe anxiety that I could not control, nor did I understand. But with the help of prayers from several people and Charlie Gerber, my counselor, I was able to defeat my anxiety and keep it at bay. What changed was the reality that I could not carry around things I could not control. I could not carry around burdens that were not mine to bear. I had to learn to jettison the junk out of my life and focus on my own spiritual life and direction.

This devotional book in part is the learning curve I had to make in the path to recovery. I also learned if others can apply the beginning principles that they will be able to make the necessary changes in their lives as well. They are simple, practical things they can do in order to change the way they think and ultimately behave.

I want to say a big thank you to my wife who gave me something I needed at the time, but did not realize it at the moment, tough love. I found that tough love along with learning to let go of my past and the things I could not control set me free. As a result, I discovered ways to grow up and out of anxiety, as well as ways to improve my life in other areas.

It does not matter where you are in your faith. We all need to perform some self-reflection and discover ways to improve our lives. May the Lord bless you as you take this thirty-day journey to improve the way you think, in order to get rid of things you no longer need. Stick with it and see how God uses what you may not know about yourself to improve your thinking.

Day 1- Beginning

Proverbs 3:5-8 Trust in the LORD with all your heart, and lean not on your own understanding; (6) In all your ways acknowledge Him, And He shall direct your paths. (7) Do not be wise in your own eyes; Fear the LORD and depart from evil. (8) It will be health to your flesh, And strength to your bones.

  My grandfather and grandmother were hoarders. American Pickers would consider them collectors, but hoarders have to justify their obscene droves of things that they have been collecting over the years. Things they had in their possession had not been touched in years maybe even decades. They are rusty, covered in animal feces, and let us not talk about the smell. I can imagine that most people can relate to these images. You may know someone that struggles with this habit of buying things. They do not need them and instead of getting rid of them, but they hold onto them thinking they have value. The truth is, the majority of it is junk.

  This study is going to dig into the junk we carry around. Things that we know we needed to get rid of a long time ago. However, we hold onto it because letting go means letting go of a part of ourselves. That is a scary thought for a lot of people. Because letting go of those things makes us feel somehow emptier. The truth is we have become emptier, but when we make room, we also have an opportunity to fill it with something else. The temptation might be to fill it with some more useless items. Things we feel will add some missing piece to our lives. However, they just add to the pile of useless relics. Having a hundred flat-head screwdrivers will never be useful if you only need one Philips-head screwdriver. If you fill your life with junk instead of the necessary tools you need to live, you may have a lot of stuff. However, it does nothing for you except add to the clutter, and the clutter is the issue. We must Jettison the Junk.

Questions:

1. What are some things in your life you would consider junk?
2. Are there things others have pointed out to you that you may need to address?
3. What are some ways you are going to prepare your heart and mind for this study?

Day 2- Let Go

Ecclesiastes 11:10 Therefore remove sorrow from your heart, and put away evil from your flesh, for childhood and youth are vanity.

  Learning to let go is one of the most difficult things for a lot of people, including myself, to do. We know in our hearts we need to change, but making the change can be a lot more difficult than it sounds. In theory, a person should be able to let it go. However, there is baggage that goes along with those decisions that you have made. A worthless piece of junk could be extremely valuable to you, based upon the memories that are attached to it. When someone dies, it is not uncommon for a person to leave things where his/her spouse or child left them. By disturbing them, you are somehow severing the person from the object.

 When we talk about jettisoning the junk, we are not talking about removing the memory, but instead understanding that the past is the past and for us to move on, we must be willing to let go of the past. Even though it may be hard, it is necessary in order to make the changes that will help us grow. You must be willing to clean the room of the person who died. You have to be willing to part with the thing that may have value to you, long with those thousand other things that you have collected. The first step which is the hardest step is to be willing to let go. Start with one thing. Make the decision to get rid of it, then simply let it go. Letting go of something that has been holding you back is freeing and empowering.

1. Name something that needs to be let go.
2. What is one way that you can change the way you look at it?
3. Make a plan of letting it go and see it through.

Day 3- Hold On

1Timothy 6:12 Fight the good fight of faith, lay hold on eternal life, to which you were also called and have confessed the good confession in the presence of many witnesses.

When I think of the topic of holding on, I think back to the song by Wilson Philips, "Hold On." In the opening lyrics of the song it states, "I know there is pain. Why do you lock yourself up in these chains? No one can change your life except for you. Don't ever let anyone step all over you." When I was dealing with anxiety, this song helped me through a lot. For good reason, it reminded me that tomorrow brings a new day. Even though I was struggling today, it did not automatically mean that I was going to be struggling tomorrow. That is the cycle we get ourselves locked into believing. I think sometimes we take the philosophy of Eeyore, who always looked at life through the eyes of the negative. Negatives are such a small portion of our lives, yet we find ourselves focusing on them.

Why do we subject ourselves to such a lie. People will take these defeats personally, store them up and use them to tell themselves they are not worthy. Hence, why a lot of people refuse to change. As we mentioned in the last lesson people hold on to the memories that keep them trapped. However, those things do not reveal the truth. The truth is you are worthy of more than what you think you are. If Jesus thought you good enough to die, He sees a value that you do not see in yourself. Letting go of your past is imperative. To do this effectively, you must hold onto the things that really matter. You cannot change the past, so why try. Hold on to the fact that you are deeply and amazingly loved. Tomorrow is not today. Every day that we live, and every action that we take is another chance at getting it right. I think of any professional that is good at their work. They did not get that way overnight. There was a lot of failures and a lot of failed attempts that riddled their path. From time to time, they will make mistakes. The difference between someone who has elevated themselves to that level and those at the bottom struggling to make it is they know the next right step to take. The past mistake is behind them and the next move to make it right is ahead of them.

1. Name 5 specific things that happened to you today that were good/ positive? (This may be harder than you think)
2. Name 3 things that you need to let go?
3. Name 3 things in your faith that got you through a difficult time? How has that changed your life/perspective.

Day 4- Moving Forward

Philippians 3:12-13…I press on, that I may lay hold of that for which Christ Jesus has also laid hold of me. Brethren, I do not count myself to have apprehended; but one thing I do, forgetting those things which are behind and reaching forward to those things which are ahead…

    One of the most iconic scenes in the movie, "The Patriot" was when the Colonial Army was being pushed back and the soldiers began to retreat. However, the main character continued to push forward, even though everyone else wanted to quit. When they saw some people were willing to push onward, and when it seemed like all hope was lost, they mustered whatever strength they had and pushed onward to give the British army one of their first major defeats in battle. Even though the story itself is fiction, the idea of pushing forward when you feel hopeless is not. There is a spiritual battle that is going on inside all of us. The natural tendency is to give up, and lay down when it seems like you have no chance to make it. However, sometimes that is when you must buckle down the most. John Wooden said, "Adversity is the state in which man most easily becomes acquainted with himself."

    Difficulties do and will arise, but when they do, how do we handle them? Do we give up because it is too hard? Do we strap in and prepare for the road ahead, knowing it is not going to be easy? Some of the most beautiful scenery is not found on the highways of life; it is found on the road less traveled.

When you refuse to deal with difficult situations, it defines your views. It defines your attitude towards pain and growth. Yes, I meant pain and growth. When you struggle, no matter what it is, you find that you grow because you learned something valuable about yourself. Maybe you found you have more strength than you realized. Maybe you found that you need to work on some areas where your life has not been up to par. Regardless, you will never know unless you choose to take the road less traveled. Push yourself somewhere you do not want to go. You must be willing to let go of your past, hold onto the things that are important, and push ahead, knowing that road is well worth the risk.

1. What things have stopped you in the past from moving forward?
2. List three areas that you know need work. (If you say you have none, you have one already, being honest with yourself.)
3. What fears are keeping you from taking that step down a difficult road?
4. Make a plan to deal with those fears.

Day 5 Taking a Risk

Proverbs 3:5-6 Trust in the LORD with all your heart, and lean not on your own understanding; (6) In all your ways acknowledge Him, And He shall direct your paths.

     A few years ago, Carla and I were boating on the lake near our house and we saw some cliff divers who were jumping off the ledge. Several of the kids had jumped into the water, but there was one young man who could not make the leap. He would run up and then stop just before he had to jump. He did this several times, all while his friends were encouraging him to jump. He finally got the courage to take the plunge. He ran, closed his eyes tight, and took the leap off the cliff into the water. Although I do not condone this kind of behavior, I do think there is a lesson to be learned from that young man. If you never take a risk, you will never experience anything beyond what you already know.

     Trusting in the Lord is a leap of faith. You do not always know where faith is going to take you, but you will end up exactly where you need to be. Risk taking is about getting yourself out of the way. More specifically it is getting your excuses out of the way. Think about all the missed opportunities that you may have had because you were afraid to take a risk. The people who refuse to take risks will never experience life beyond what they already know. Change is necessary, and with change comes risk, and with risk can come reward. What if it fails? Failures are nothing more than learning experiences of what not to do. You cannot let the fear of failure keep you from living. Otherwise, you will never grow out of the hole where you have sheltered yourself.

Risks are by design not guaranteed, at least in our eyes they are not. Trusting in the Lord may not seem like a risk, but if it causes us to get out of our comfort zone, it absolutely is going to take a leap of faith on our part. It means we are going to have to change, with change comes discomfort, and discomfort creates resistance, and resistance creates a desire to quit. This is the moment a person must choose how to move forward. Change means a change of mind, and that means work both in ourselves and with the choices we have made. Churches get stuck in these ruts because the people in the church are afraid of risks and/or change. If you want to get rid of the bad habits and make some serious changes, you must be willing to take risks. You are going to have to take that leap of faith in which you can never go back to the person you are now. You will become something different. Even if you fail, if you learned from the experience, you are better for it

1. Name a couple risks you did not take but you wish you would have.
2. What risks do you know you need to take now?
3. Name some things that keep you from being a risk taker.
4. Start thinking about how you are going to overcome them.

Day 6- Developing a Plan

Proverbs 21:5 The plans of the diligent lead surely to plenty, but those of everyone who is hasty, surely to poverty.

This step in the process is where most people fail. There is an old expression, if you fail to plan, you plan to fail. You cannot succeed in anything by chance. You must plan it out and works towards it. That is easily said, but not easily done for most people. Planning is intentional, it is purposeful, and it is driven by a desire to see a change take place. When you go to remodel your house, or build a house, you do not go into that project haphazardly. You hire an architect, and tell him some of the features you want. He takes those general ideas and builds a blueprint that makes a very deliberate and purposeful layout of how it is going to be built.

We talked about taking risks. Risks are not without at least a measure of planning. You weigh all your options, you look at what it will cost you, and when you are ready, you take that leap and do it. Going back to the cliff jumper illustration, you are taking a risk jumping into water from a cliff, but if you do not know the area before you jump, you are taking an unnecessary risk that has a high probability of failure. Risks are necessary, but not without some planning.

Planning is a crucial part of the walk with the Lord. Think how long it took for God to send the Messiah. It was done with careful planning, and more importantly, perfect timing. If you move before you are prepared to move, two things will likely happen; you will fail miserably and wonder why you took the risk, which will hurt your chances of taking another risk. It will likely cost you more than you anticipated, and you might end up spiritually spent before you get started. There is the unlikely chance that you get lucky and you come out on the other side unscathed, however, that is not the normal, so do not think it will work out. People will bet their lives away on lottery tickets on the rare chance they might get lucky. That is not, nor should it be, the Christian philosophy on getting spiritually rich.

  Instead, careful planning is the key to start out on the journey of real and effective change. To this point, we have talked about letting go of the things that hold you back, holding onto the things that matter, moving forward, and taking risks, but up to this point we had not dealt with putting it all together. Over the course of the next few days, we will deal with more specific ways that plan for real and effectual change in your life that will make you a better Christian and a better follower of Jesus.

1. What kinds of changes do you want to make in your life?
2. Why do you think people refuse to plan for the changes they want?
3. How have you fallen into that cycle of traps of not planning? How are you planning to change it?

4. What is some of biggest excuses that most people give when they refuse to plan?

Day 7- Be a Visionary

Proverbs 29:18 Without a Vision the People will Perish

Developing a plan is an essential part of moving from and beyond our past. It first must start with a vision. Without a vision, knowing where you are going becomes chaotic. How are you going to get from point A to point B must be well thought out before you can move. Before the invention of the GPS, people were forced to use road maps to plan out their destination. I can remember my dad spending two days looking over the trip. Memorizing roads that we needed to take, so that he had good sense of how to get there. A vision helps to create that starting point. It is not the roads you are going to take or the actual traveling you will do. It is the map. The vision lays out the ground rules of what makes up the plan. There are several questions when planning a trip; are we traveling by car or by plane, and perhaps, depending on where you live and your destination, by boat? It helps to draft out the budget by stating the parameters of what you are willing to spend. The vision is the foundation of what you want to build. To use another illustration, when a person plans for retirement, a person must determine what they want their retirement to look like. Does the person want to travel? What does that person want to do once they stop working? The vision will guide their financial decisions.

When we talk about jettisoning the junk, what does that mean for you? Are you only interested in tidying up your life, or do you need a more radical change? What are some things you would like to see at the end of all of it? The vision must establish the basic, although generalized goals you wish to see happen. But the most important thing about the vision is the follow through. If you are willing to set up the vision, you must be willing to stick to the defining principles of it.

You might be thinking, I do not need to do this. I will figure it out along the way. Being both in the secular field and in the ministry, winging it does two things: it wastes valuable time and resources, and it is more likely to lead to discouragement and failure. Visions are an important, if not the most important part of the plan. If you fail to set up a vision (parameters) of your lifestyle change, then you will struggle finding direction. If you do not set up a vision of where you hope to be, how will you ever know if you have accomplished it? If you do not set up a vision, how can you properly audit your progress?

A final thought on this. A vision can be broken or altered if you realize your vision was pointed in the wrong way, or you were lacking a critical component to it. Visions set the course, but changes will come and you will need to become adaptable to those changing situations. We will discuss this later in more detail. Be willing to set the vision. Be willing to hold to the vision. Be willing to look at the vision as you progress through the process and make changes as necessary.

1. A vision should include things you wish to accomplish. List a few items you wish to accomplish.
2. Visions are generally built into one or two sentences. Write out your vision statement that points out what you want to do or work upon. Ex. Over the course of the next year, I want to deepen my relationship with God, enrich my relationship with others, and become a better disciple of Jesus.
3. Spend some time in prayer and seek out council to see if your vision is either too broad or too narrow, and if it includes all the elements of what you plan to do.

Day 8- Prioritizing the Details

Matthew 22:35-37 Then one of them, a lawyer, asked Him a question, testing Him, and saying, (36) "Teacher, which is the great commandment in the law?" (37) Jesus said to him, 'YOU SHALL LOVE THE LORD YOUR GOD WITH ALL YOUR HEART, WITH ALL YOUR SOUL, AND WITH ALL YOUR MIND.'

    When we talk about getting rid of the junk and making positive changes. We must prioritize what is most important. When you are cleaning out a house riddled with garbage, you do not go to the back of the house and work your way forward. You must deal with the mess that is right in front of you. The vision has been set, you know what you want to do, now it is time to prioritize the vision. If the vision is going to take several steps to fulfill, you cannot start at the last step and say you are done. There is a process you must go through. It is like the prefabricated furniture that you can buy. Each step of the process has a reason. It may not necessarily make sense at the beginning, but there is generally a reason for the steps you are taking. If you skip steps, you might find yourself missing important parts of the build that will take away from the original design.

    Prioritizing life choices can make the difference between success and failure. If you want to take a trip, and you leave before you are financially able to make the trip. It may cause you to get stranded or to miss out on things that you really wanted to see and/or do. The need to make sure what you are doing is done in an appropriate order may, and often does, affect your ability to make the necessary changes. Take it from a person that has done this too many times and has learned by the school of hard knocks. Prioritizing your life choices is essential to making good choices. It reminds me of a credit card. Credit cards can be one of two things for individuals. They can be great assets that can work for you, or they can be a bane to your existence. The average credit card debt is around $20,000. The reason for tragedy has been due to the urge for the instant gratification. Credit cards allow people to buy things they cannot afford. It leads to poor decision making because people do not stop to consider if it is a good idea. It is based off the emotion.

  Priorities should rarely, if ever, be based upon feeling. Instead, priorities must be based on what exists. I am reminded of the scriptures that mention a king will not go to war before he has counted the cost, or a person build a house before he counted the cost. You must stop and consider, "do I need it right now, or can I wait?" Some things do need our immediate action; some can wait but still need our attention; still others are things that you want, but you do not need. If you are going to change your life, then you must work on the things that need your attention now. If you are living in sin, this needs to be addressed first before you can work on other areas of your life. Do not focus on the wants that can take our attention away from the end goals. Most people want the here and now. The newest trends and the newest gadgets flood the market, and people are convinced they need them. They will spend their money they needed to pay for bills, groceries, or repairs on these items and wonder why they ae in constant trouble. It is easy to get caught up in this cycle, but if want to change we must break it.

1. Make a list of things you know needs work. List them in three categories High, medium and low. (If you are dealing with a sin. It must be number 1 on the list.)
2. Spend time in prayer and confide in a friend to see if you have labelled your priorities in the proper category. Real immediate priorities sometimes get muffled by our own prejudices.
3. Once you have worked it out prepare to act.

Day 9- Prepare to Act

Genesis 12:1-2 Now the LORD had said to Abram: "Get out of your country, from your family and from your father's house, to a land that I will show you. (2) I will make you a great nation; I will bless you and make your name great; And you shall be a blessing.

  Change does not happen because someone desires to change. You must be willing to act. You can create a vision statement, you can prioritize your goals, but until you are willing to act on them, your plans will always fail. This is where the rubber meets the road. If you have ever seen a plane approaching the ground, you can always know the point of contact when a plane touches it. The plume of smoke is unmistakable. A person can pretend up to the point that action is involved. You will find out how serious he is when it comes down to carrying out his plans. Nine days after writing this lesson, people will be looking for a change in the new year. Gym memberships will skyrocket and people will invest in exercise equipment. For the majority of the people who make these decisions, they will start out going to the gym or using their machine, but within 3-4 weeks the equipment starts collecting dust and the doors of the gyms are rarely used.

  Talk is cheap unless you can back it up. Excuses are often used to justify our reasoning to quit. I am too busy. It is too hard. It is not what I expected. You name it, people have said it. Let's be honest, we have probably been guilty of it. I know I have. Dealing with anxiety and overcoming it was no easy task. It was the hardest thing I ever did. I had to look deep and realize I was the cause of the anxiety. I created it, and I had to be the one that dealt with it. Thankfully I did not like the medicine they put me on, and I realized medicine was only a band-aid for the real issue at hand. My repressed anger, hurt and guilt over things I could not control all came to a head, breaking like a dam that had lost its integrity. Overwhelmed and broken, I had to make a choice. I could either deal with it, or live with it.

      This devotional book is the result of the choices I had to make. I chose to deal with it and confront my demons head on. If I can do it, so can you. Life is made up of choices and actions. You can choose to be who you are even though you do not like what you have become, or you can choose to act. Action requires work, and work requires commitment. If you are going to lose weight, you are not going to do it by talking about it. Actions are required. I have talked about taking a risk, and this is where the risk comes into play. You can make all the plans in the world, but until you make the first step, then the second and continue carrying them out there is no risk. There is no real change until you take that leap from words to actions. Until you can take that leap, all the planning in the world will get you nowhere.

1. How do you plan to turn your words into actions?

2. Answer honestly why your plans have failed in the past?
3. What did you learn and how will this time be different?
4. Don't quit or make excuses when things get tough because they will.

Day- 10 First step

Matthew 17:20 So Jesus said to them, "Because of your unbelief; for assuredly, I say to you, if you have faith as a mustard seed, you will say to this mountain, 'Move from here to there,' and it will move; and nothing will be impossible for you.

There was a commercial years ago advertising the need to start investing. The people would say, "I do not know where to start" and an arrow would show up at their feet and say, "start here." Taking that first step is always the hardest to make because you are crossing into the unknown. Samwise Gamgee said in the Fellowship of the Ring, "If I take one more step it is the furthest from home I've ever been." Sam was not saying I am unwilling to go. Instead what he meant was, from here on, I do not know where I am going.

The unknown is where people struggle. The what if questions, and the excuses always make their way into our minds. However, we must be willing to lay that all aside in order to move. Going back to the cliff illustration, that first step is the move that transitions you from where you were to a totally different environment and a different mindset. Knowing that you can do something really changes your outlook. It changes how you will approach it the next time. The next step is not so hard because the worst part is over. It reminds me of my first time on a roller coaster, and perhaps you can relate. You are full of fear as you wait, but now it is your turn, and the unknown is about to become the known, whether you are ready or not. The bar is lowered, the announcements are made, and then begins the long, arduous climb as the cars are pulled up the hill. The sound of clicking is heard from the track, and you feel restless on the inside. There is no backing out now. You are strapped in, and ready or not, the car begins the descent down the hill, along with it begins the best 30 seconds of your life, for you experience a thrill like no other.

    Like the coaster, you must be willing to step out on faith. Stop wasting time making excuses and move. Stop saying you cannot because you can. You must move to change, and yes, change is hard. Israel, when they left Egypt, grumbled because they struggled to deal with their new lives outside of slavery. Some even desired to go back to the old life because the change was hard. No one ever said that the road to a new life would be one easily travelled. However, the road to change is worth it. When I had to make the first real step to change my life, post anxiety, it was hard. I had a lot of support, but ultimately, no one could move for me. I had to move. I had to take the first step. I had to say I cannot live the way I've been living and live for Jesus as I should. That first step led to a long, arduous move up the hill of change. But once I got a glimpse of the other side, it changed my life forever. I realized that the trip was worth it, even though I did not want to make it. I want to tell you, if I could do it, you can do it too. Never underestimate the strength that you possess when you are serving a God who has the power to heal the sick, make the lame to walk, and calm the raging storms. Let go of your fear and move. Trust that the Lord knows what He is doing, step out on faith and let God work in your obedient steps towards a better life with Him.

1. I challenge you to make that first step out on faith to trust that God has a plan for you and He will bless your efforts even if you cannot see them immediately.
2. If you have not started this habit, purchase a notebook or a journal, and start to write down your journey with the Lord. This will help you see the progress you have made.

Day 11- Not if But When

Psalms 9:9-11 The LORD also will be a refuge for the oppressed, A refuge in times of trouble. (10) And those who know Your name will put their trust in You; For You, LORD, have not forsaken those who seek You. (11) Sing praises to the LORD, who dwells in Zion! Declare His deeds among the people.

Troubles are going to come. It is not a matter of if, but when they will happen. For so many people, they try their hardest to avoid trouble, when sometimes all they can do is face it. Today I want you to focus on this one truth. You are going to face trouble, and it will get hard. But you can endure it and come out on the other side better as a result. Running from trouble does not deal with it. All you are doing is delaying the inevitable confrontation, and by putting it off, more times than not you compound it. If you delay dealing with complications, often what happens is all the other things you cannot face will rear their ugly heads all at the same time. Running only makes you more exhausted. People do not like confrontations. They would rather be silent than to tell someone that they have a problem with them. In private they are warriors willing to defeat the enemy, but in public they just cannot find the same courage. So, they are like Snaggle Puss, when he would say, "exit, stage right."

We are taught fight or flight as a natural reaction to danger, but we have translated that reaction to mean run away from all troubles. We are taught to pick our battles, but more often than not we do not fight at all. Instead, we let the issues that we struggle with overwhelm us. We let the enemy surround us. In that moment of being surrounded, we finally decide to act out of pure desperation, or we surrender and give up. That is why confronting battles early can turn the tide. We are going to still face those same issues, but we do not have to do so backed into a corner. We do not have to fight all our battles at once.

"You don't know what I have done." You are right I don't, but I know what I've done. I know from experience, not facing the situation head on has ever solved my problems. Fear keeps us from dealing with things we must face. You want to change, now it is time to face your demons. You will never grow from your past if you cannot face it. It takes strength and courage, but you are not alone. You have a God who desires to help you deal with it. You also have people who will stand by your side through it.

1. What battles have you been avoiding that you know you need to face?
2. Why have you run from them before?
3. What are you going to do this time that is different from before?

Part 2

To this point, we have looked at a very structured approach on how to move forward, and I believe that structure is one of the most necessary things to success. If you do not have structure, you are like a one-legged duck. You move around a lot, but you do not get anywhere. However, from this point forward we are not going to be as structured. Instead, we are going to look at some important things that we need to learn, but they will not necessarily have a particular order. This section will deal with more individual things to consider and think upon as you progress in your journey to become a better follower of Jesus.

Day 12

Mark 7:3 For the Pharisees and all the Jews do not eat unless they wash their hands in a special way, holding the tradition of the elders.

If we are going to talk about change, then I think the first place that we must start is talking about traditions. They can be a good thing, as long as they are based upon the Bible, or they draw a family close together in the Lord. But traditions can also be extremely hindering as well. They can stop ingenuity. They can create apathy, carelessness, and recklessness. Traditions can keep people from growing and pursing after a relationship with the Lord.

Mark chapter 7 starts with the Pharisees looking at the disciples with disgust because they would not wash their hands according to the traditions. These were not Biblical traditions, but to the religious leaders of the day, these traditions were equal to the written word of God. When a tradition makes you judge something with a slanted view, when it keeps you from learning and growing, it gets in the way of true faith. The first real changes in our lives comes when we take a good, hard look at ourselves and discover what traditions that we might possess that keep us away from the Lord. Jesus calls them out, "you honor Me with your lips, but your hearts are far from Me."

If you want to change your life to follow the Lord, think hard on the traditions you have created, and ask are they helping or hurting. This is something only you can answer, and you must be honest with yourself. If they are inhibiting you from going out on faith and trusting in the Lord, it is time to rethink them. If these traditions have caused you to give up things you should be honoring, it is time to purge them in order to be obedient to the Lord.

The Pharisees had created a system where they controlled every aspect of their lives. What it created was a people who cared more about honoring the traditions than honoring God. When Jesus went against them, the Pharisees did not recite from the Bible, instead, they cited the traditions Jesus and his disciples violated. The Pharisees felt dishonored because someone dared to challenge them according to their traditions. It was personal to them, and Jesus took and revealed their heart to them. He showed them how far they had fallen. The biggest lesson I have learned from Jesus and traditions: never let a tradition get in the way of your faithfulness to God.

1. What are some traditions that have kept you from Jesus in the past?
2. What things can you do in order to stop developing bad traditions?

Day 13

Proverbs 6:6-8 Go to the ant, you sluggard! Consider her ways and be wise, which, having no captain, Overseer, or ruler, provides her supplies in the summer, and gathers her food in the harvest.

 I love to hunt, especially hunting deer, but hunting around here in the state of Indiana is not that hard to do. The hardest part, usually, is finding a good place to hunt. Deer hunting generally consist of going into the woods around August, finding good deer paths, and setting up stands where you believe you have a good chance of finding them. But hunting for elk in places like Colorado is a lot different. You must be prepared to move where they are, and you will be doing so in air saturations much lower than what you find in the Midwest. You must make sure your heart and your lungs can handle the trip otherwise you can literally die. It takes hard work and no one is going to force you to do it. It is not something you do by going to the gym once a week or by starting to get ready two weeks before the trip. It takes months of preparation to make sure you are ready to go.

 When it comes to spiritual growth, you must be like the elk hunter. The need to be prepared in service to the Lord is a serious endeavor. You cannot take it lightly. Part of training your life for the road ahead is making sure you do not do too, much too fast. We, as people, tend to go overboard when we are doing something. We start out too hard, and it is too much so we quit. Starting out small and working your way up takes time and patience. Look at the ants. It takes them all summer to prepare for winter. If you are preparing for the long haul, you must train your mind and your body for the road ahead. You must set goals and shoot for them. If you reach them, great, but if you do not, then do not give up. Work towards them with a mind to complete them, and do not let distractions keep you from doing it. It has been said it takes 30 days to create a habit, but it only takes 3 to break it.

    The big thing to keep in mind is perseverance. Keep your eye focused on the end goal. Keep moving forward, and never give up. You will be amazed at how much you will grow when you focus on your goals, work toward them, and keep the promises you have made. God will bless your efforts as a result. You may not see them immediately. It often happens when you are not looking for those blessings, that you finally see the difference in your life. It is usually in the form of someone that you know seeing the difference you have made. Today, keep working toward your goal and have a desire to see it through.

1. What areas of your life do you need to focus your attention?
2. What goals do you plan to set to see them accomplished?

Day 14

Philippians 2:3-5 Let nothing be done through selfish ambition or conceit, but in lowliness of mind let each esteem others better than himself. (4) Let each of you look out not only for his own interests, but also for the interests of others. (5) Let this mind be in you which was also in Christ Jesus…

    Why do we do the things that we do? It is the big question we need to answer if we are going to change our lives to be better servants for the Lord. We must figure out our motivation. I have heard over the years, what you invest your money into are the things you care about most. I am not talking about the occasional trips to the movie theatre or to the local restaurant. I am talking about what you really invest a lot of money into. Those are the things that generally occupy our lives as well. We spend so much time focusing on the material things of this world that we sometimes forget what we are supposed to be doing. Not only that, but we tend to justify those same behaviors as normal and good. We say, "Oh, it is not that big of a deal," when in reality it is a big deal. We tell ourselves that the problems we have are not really problems. I can deal with it. I do not need the help from the Lord or anyone else. However, it is for that reason we continue to struggle.

    It takes a humble heart to admit we need help, and we need to change the way we live. Selfishness and the desire to do it ourselves often keeps us from achieving the goals we know we need to reach. Often, they keep us from trying, for we have become content with failing. It is the life of the redeemed and humble soul that begins to realize the faultiness of our struggles and the need to change. I am reminded of the movie Cars. Lightning McQueen was very much the individual this verse describes. It took him being in a town that showed him what he had been missing to realize his need to change himself. Therefore, instead of investing in things, invest in people. Invest in the lives of those who are striving to be obedient to the Lord. Invest in Christ fully and let Him lead. Invest in the word and let it change you from the inside. You are not alone, and people, if you will let them, can help you when you are struggling to draw closer to the Lord.

1. What things do you need to give up in order to live more for Christ?
2. How do you think allowing people to help you grow will help you grow?

Day 15

Proverbs 16:18 Pride goes before destruction, And a haughty spirit before a fall.

There was a sign in my elementary cafeteria that said, "You cannot make all the mistakes in the world, so learn from everyone else." I read those words every time I would go to lunch. Undoubtedly, they made an impact on my life, for I still remember the words, and I have tried to live by them. However, I am riddled with mistakes, as all of us are. This is the hard part of life. It is hard to live it perfectly. This is amplified if a person deals with pride. Pride perverts our importance in the world and the space we occupy. It causes us to think more highly of ourselves then we ought. That is what happened to the Pharisees. They were a victim of their own pride and arrogance. They believed their lives were more important than the people they represented. When Jesus challenged them on it, they got very defensive and blamed and accused Him of wrongdoing. However, they would not admit they were wrong.

Pride keeps us from seeing the truth. We are people worthy of condemnation and deserving of death. God does not need us. Instead, we need Him. We will not and cannot grow in our faith if we are full of pride. The only cure for pride is humility, and unfortunately, for many, that comes in the form of humiliation. Most people are not cured from pride without being exposed as being pride filled. This is one of the biggest issues that wreak havoc in our lives.

Moses had a pride problem. He believed he was destined to be the Savior of Israel. He took it upon himself and killed an Egyptian. As a result, he had to run for his life. The next forty years he became a shepherd, a far cry from being a man of great importance. This act humbled him, and he learned to let go of his pride. When he went back to Egypt, he was not the same man that left. He was ready to follow the Lord no matter the cost. Most people follow the same pattern. They are good for everything, and then they are good for nothing. When they are broken, they become good to go.

If we want to follow the Lord, we must be willing to let go of our pride. This is accomplished by opening ourselves to the Lord, exposing those pride issues, and jettisoning them out of our lives. We must recognize that pride is an easy trap that causes us to fall. Humility, on the other hand, creates a way for us to serve the Lord effectively. The work we do is still important, but the work is no longer about us. It is about the Lord.

1. What things can pride destroy?
2. What steps can we take to prevent pride in our lives?
3. What lessons can we learn from others to keep us away from pride?

Day 16

Psalm 16:10-11 For You will not leave my soul in Sheol, nor will You allow Your Holy One to see corruption. (11) You will show me the path of life; In Your presence is fullness of joy; At Your right hand are pleasures forevermore.

  When I was 15 years old, I spiral fractured my tibia and fibula on my left leg right above my ankle while coming off a horse. They had to do a total reconstructive surgery of my bones, but thirteen screws and a plate later I was on the mend. It was a long road to recovery, but it eventually healed, and today, outside of the scars, I would have never known I did it. It is one thing to have a broken bone. It is an entirely different thing to have a broken heart. A broken heart lingers, and the pain does not easily subside on its own. This is the reason a lot of people will resort to drugs or alcohol when they are struggling with their issues. They think if they can drown out their sorrows they will go away, but this only makes the problems worse.

  You cannot drown out the pain. People give up when they are broken, thinking they are broken beyond repair. However, being broken does not mean that you cannot be fixed. It simply means you need time to heal. You need time to process, and then, if you are willing to put in the work, you can make a recovery. Things will never be the same, but they should not be either. Loss and heartache change us, but if we use them correctly, they can change us in a good way. They remind us we are not who we were, but they can also reveal who we have become.

Pain is not the enemy of joy and growth, instead pain is a result of deep love. When we realize that point, it will help us to cope through it and come out on the other side better than we were before. Joy is not the absence of pain, rather is the outlook through the pain. It is the choice that we must be able to make. It is not easy, nor will it be fun. Instead of running from it, embrace it, take it on and find the joy that is contained within it. It is there. You just have to find it.

1. Why do you think it is so hard to find joy in pain?
2. What are some of the ways that we find joy through the pain?
3. Do not run from pain. Embrace it and find the joy hidden within it!

Day 17

Psalms 26:11 But as for me, I will walk in my integrity...

    Integrity is something no one can take from you. Instead, you must be willing to give it up. When people think about you, what kinds of things do they say? Would they say, "that person is crooked, conniving, and I would never trust him/her." Would they say, "he is nice, but he are unreliable?" Those are things we do not want to hear, and truthfully, never like to hear. A person of integrity walks differently. He/she walks in such a way that whether someone is looking or not, they are doing what they are supposed to be doing. Integrity is important in marriage, and in the workplace. It is important to the Christian in everything he/she does.

    This is the center piece of all Christian principles. It is not the most important quality. But without it, nothing else really matters. When you have integrity, your words will not have to defend you. Instead, your actions have already done it. Once you lose it, people might draw into question whether you can be trusted. That is a hard thing to get back. They will question your motives as to what you are doing. I did that with my grandfather, and even though he loved me, in that one area, he could not trust me. I was never able to win back his trust. Do not make the mistake of losing what you have. Again, you are the only one that can lose it, so do not let it go.

The greatest example of this comes from when I worked at a prison in Kentucky. I had inmates come up to me and swear by their moms, their dads, their kids, and God never to do something again. However, it was not long after that these same inmates would break their word and defame the very people they swore they would uphold. The Bible makes it very clear on how we are to handle these situations. Let your yes be yes, and your no be no. Integrity does not rely upon making promises. It is built upon how you live your life.

Do not let your integrity go. Hold onto it tight and never let it go. You will find yourself able to better serve the kingdom if you do what you say you are going to do. Do not fall into the trap of saying what you are going to do, and not fulfilling it.

1. What things have cost you your integrity in the past?
2. Why is integrity so important to the Christian walk?
3. Does having integrity change the way someone looks at you? Why?

Day 18

Ecclesiastes 10:12 The words of a wise man's mouth are gracious, But the lips of a fool shall swallow him up…

How we speak can make a big difference in the way people perceive us. We could give the greatest complement to someone, however, if it is in the wrong tone, then it could be misunderstood. That is one of the reasons that James talks about the tongue that can bless and curse. The tongue can create fires that are hard to put out. The tongue is a difficult thing to control, and if we are going to fix what is broken, fixing the way that we talk is something that needs our attention.

The question we need to ask ourselves is, does our language build up or tear down. You might be thinking, we are told to exhort and correct people. That is true, but it does not mean that you must beat someone down with your words. Like raising kids, you do not want to acerbate someone while trying to correct them. Correction is meant to change behavior, and if our words are full of venom, we will not change anything. Think back to the way people treated you with harsh words and how it cut deep. It is extremely painful to have someone hurt us with words. We have heard the lie from so many people over the years, "sticks and stones may break my bones, but words will never hurt me." The opposite is true. Words cut deep and they hurt worse. Broken bones are much easier to heal than a broken heart and a broken spirit.

When you speak, what and how you are speaking will impact the way people respond to you. If we are going to grow up in the faith, controlling our words and controlling our tone must be something we cannot leave behind or put off. Words have power and what we put behind them matters. We can either fill them with love, or we can fill them with venom. I do not know about you, but I want to do the former.

1. How did it feel the last time someone said something hurtful to you?
2. How did it feel the last time you said a hurtful thing to someone else?
3. Why does tone play such an important role in language, and in what ways can changing the tone change the way people perceive our message?

Day 19

1 Corinthians 15:33 Do not let anyone fool you. Bad people can make those who want to live good become bad. NLT

If bad company corrupts good morals, then good company builds up already established morals. Establishing a baseline of friends that truly care about you and want the very best for you helps develop your relationship with the Lord. We automatically think if we stay away from people who live in depravity, that will help us grow closer to the Lord. However, there is another group of people we need to try and avoid. These people are the negative influencers in our lives. These are the people that complain about everything. They drain the joy right out of you because they do not have any themselves. If you are a person who always sees the worst in everything, you cannot find the positive in anything. To be fair, I can be one of those people, for I grew up in an environment that was full of negativity. I get it. It is easy to get caught up in those moments, and everyone has them, but negativity can a pit that we choose to live in. It is dark, and we do not want to be alone, so we convince people to join us in the pit. When someone tries to pull us out, we may instead try to pull them into it.

Negativity destroys relationships because it is singularly focused. It cannot see the broader scope outside of its view. It would be like looking through a paper towel roll. Your scope is limited by your vision. All you see is the negative. I heard a wise man once say that 95% of all the things that happen to us are good, but we tend to focus on the 5% that impacts us negatively. We live there. Someone pulls out in front of us and that could ruin our day. Someone brings up a sore memory, and it bothers you all day if you choose to focus on it. We could give example after example of the kinds of things people will let negatively affect them.

However, those are choices, and we must be willing to let them go. Jesus died for our sins. He gave us freedom apart from them. We have been given a new life, and we get to be a part of it. That is amazing, and we should choose joy as a result. I want to stop here and emphasize the fact that joy is a choice. It is not an emotion that comes and goes at the whim of every bad situation. Joy is something we must incorporate into our lives. It is such an important aspect that Paul mentions it as part of the fruit of the Spirit. Without joy, life in Christ is meaningless. Joy removes all reasons to despair, for you see beyond the medial problems and embrace the big picture of eternity with Jesus.

1. In what ways have you let negative situations or people drag you down?
2. How do you recover from a negative situation or conversation?
3. How can you best apply this lesson to your life?

Day 20

Matthew 6:22-24 "The lamp of the body is the eye. If therefore your eye is good, your whole body will be full of light. (23) But if your eye is bad, your whole body will be full of darkness. If therefore the light that is in you is darkness, how great is that darkness! (24) "No one can serve two masters; for either he will hate the one and love the other, or else he will be loyal to the one and despise the other. You cannot serve God and mammon.

What you choose to look at does affect your life, whether you would like to admit it or not. Our eyes give us a vision into a world that we see. But what you allow your eyes to see will affect you depending on what you choose to look at. Our eyes stimulate the body into action based on what we see. It could also create fear depending on how you are seeing it.

I am not a huge fan of heights. For me, looking on the edge of a cliff would not be something I would enjoy, but for others, that experience is amazing. The reason that it is different is how we stimulate our eyes and our minds to think. If we view something as being scary, our eyes will see it as scary because our mind tells us it is. If our mind is convinced it is good, we will be more attracted to it. When we go out to eat, the first thing we will judge is how the food looks. If it does not look good, we have a harder time eating it.

That translates into our spiritual life as well. If something looks good to you, you will be more inclined to look at it more. For someone who has grown up objectifying the opposite sex, they may not see anything wrong with viewing someone else in provocative clothing. However, if it is not something you are used to seeing, it may come across as offensive. However, our eyes can become callous to the things we see. If we like what we see, and we justify looking at it even though we know it is wrong, our eyes will want to gravitate to it. Therefore, so many men in the church have struggled with pornography. It is not that they want to do it. They know it is wrong, but their eyes have become callous to it, and what your eyes become callous to, your mind will callous as well.

      You cannot control your environment all the time, but you can control your eyes. You must keep your eyes pure, for they see things that Satan likes to use against us. If you have struggled with alcohol, do not be around people who drink, for your eyes see what you used to do, and you could be drawn back into it. If you struggle with eating, going down the snack isle may not be a good thing for you. If you struggle with lust, going to a place where people dress provocatively may not be the place for you. You must train your eyes to see differently. Your eyes do not control you, instead you control your eyes. They will follow what you allow them to follow, and they will focus on what you allow them to focus. This is one of the hardest things to do, but it is also one of the most essential things a Christian must undertake in order to get His life right with Jesus.

1. In what ways can we control what we see?
2. How can vision be blinded for a Christian?
3. What can you do to control a situation with your eyes when it is not in your control?

Day 21

James 3:8-10 But no man can tame the tongue. It is an unruly evil, full of deadly poison. (9) With it we bless our God and Father, and with it we curse men, who have been made in the similitude of God. (10) Out of the same mouth proceed blessing and cursing. My brethren, these things ought not to be so.

Be careful little mouth what you say. Another verse from that familiar song resonates with those who are willing to hear it. Words can either build up or tear down. I think of the kid that tells himself that he is no good, or the man who says God cannot love him after what he has done. I think of the mother, when the baby cannot stop crying, what a failure she believes she is. So many words in our language; so many things we can say. How are we using our words?

I think of the teacher that tells his student, "You will never amount to anything." I think of the parent that tells his children, "If you do not stop, you are going to end up in prison one day." I think of the preacher who condemns the congregation because they did not approve of his program. These all happen, and they all carry with them a burden that cannot be easily removed once they have been placed. Words have power, and words can destroy. We are not rubber, and words do not just bounce right off. They often stick to us. These same words often hurt worse than a broken bone.

We, as Christians, are called to be different. We are called to use our words with compassion and mercy. We are to use our words with the attitude to exalt and to build up, not to tear down.

If we want to change our perspective and get rid of some of the junk we are carrying around, we need to learn to speak differently. People are going to frustrate us, they are going to hurt us, they are going to make mistakes, and they are going to fail. We do not need to pile it on by tearing them down with our words.

The same goes when we fail, we cannot tear ourselves down every time we fail. We must learn to take the experience, speak words of encouragement, and try to do it right next time. I can only imagine men like Edison, when they failed. I would like to think they said when it didn't work, "Well, that didn't work let's try something different." Men and women who are innovators can do what they do because failure is only a learning experience and not the end of it all. Do not let the words that come out of your mouth become poison to others or to yourself. Do not subject yourself to other's poison. It only makes you sick, and if you allow it, it will kill your faith. Choose instead to breed healthy and productive relationships.

1. What ways can we breed healthy and productive relationships?

2. What kinds of ways can we or others spew poison?
3. What things can we do different to see this accomplished?

Day 22

Acts 2:37 Now when they heard this, they were cut to the heart, and said to Peter and the rest of the apostles, "Men and brethren, what shall we do?"

This is a very familiar passage for a lot of different reasons. I think of the context of which this was written. This was a truly momentous occasion; the church would start because of these people. This was the first response to a call of Jesus since He had died, was buried, and rose again. These people, up to this point, had rejected the Lord as being the Messiah. They could not see who He really was. But the sermon Peter preached, and through the working of the Holy Spirit, it all came to light for them. They cried out in response these famous words.

Responding to the call of Christ is a very important action that everyone must face. Some are going to accept it. Others are going to reject it. Still others are going to ride the fence. But everyone is going to respond to the gospel in one way or another.

The one thing we do not want to do, however, is react to the gospel. What I mean when I use that word is simple. Reactions are not thought out. They are done for the moment and then easily not fulfilled. I think of the seed Jesus talks about that is thrown in shallow soil. It grows up fast and then withers away about as fast. Reactions are not meant to last, but that is how most people live their lives today. It is about those momentary moments and not the long-term commitments.

A response requires some thinking, a response requires some conviction, but a response also requires some action. Otherwise, it is nothing more than a reaction. It reminds me of the people that switch their favorite teams based upon who is winning that year. The true fans stay with their team even if their team stinks.

How do you respond to God? Have you ever thought about it that way? Think about your life and when you grew the most. Think about the times you were most dedicated. I guarantee it was when you were the most committed to God. You took God's word to heart, and you did something about it. You did not hear a message and shelve it as just another thing you heard. You took it to heart, and you moved with it. That is how we are to respond. This verse today would be nothing unless they acted upon what they were told to do. 3,000 people responded to the message, because they took to heart what they heard. They thought about it. Then they responded to it.

1. Today, I want to challenge you to think about how you have responded to Jesus lately.
2. In what ways can you improve your response to Jesus?
3. In what ways have you done well?

Day 23

1Timothy 6:6-10 Now godliness with contentment is great gain. (7) For we brought nothing into this world, and it is certain we can carry nothing out. (8) And having food and clothing, with these we shall be content. (9) But those who desire to be rich fall into temptation and a snare, and into many foolish and harmful lusts which drown men in destruction and perdition. (10) For the love of money is a root of all kinds of evil, for which some have strayed from the faith in their greediness, and pierced themselves through with many sorrows.

In the Book, <u>Man in the Mirror</u> by Patrick Morley, he talks about the lack of contentment that has been bred into our society. When this book was written, it was true but has become even more true today. We live in a throwaway society. Nothing has value because nothing is expected to last. We consume more now than any other time in history, with the home delivery services that are available, the consumption has continued to rise.

We desire to have the newest and greatest things. But newer and greater does not always equate better. The newer vehicles are harder to work on because the engineers moved things that used to be easily accessible into places that are much harder to reach. They want you to buy the newest model, and they will convince you this year is better than the last. They pressure you into borrowing money you do not have to pay for things you do not need. It ultimately puts pressure on you to do things you would not normally do to make ends meet.

This equates to faith as well. We live in a society that is driven by secular humanism. As a result, we buy into things that do not even matter. Things like sports and TV shows, and digital devices have dominated our lives. We talk more about the latest marvel movie, or the last episode of our favorite show. Our heroes have become fictional characters like Ironman and Captain America. Instead of men that have quite literally transformed the world like Einstein or Newton.

Contentment, we have learned from society, is not possible. However, we should desire it. Not being overloaded with anything should be something good, yet we lost the ability to see it. The question is why? We are too busy trying to please people that do not care, than pleasing our God who really does care. You may not ever be known or have something new and that is okay. But having a sound relationship with your family, with your friends, and with your God does make all the difference in the world. You came in with nothing you will leave with nothing. Why not invest in the things that really matter, make them a priority, and pursue them and leave everything else where they belong, necessary but not important.

1. Why do you think contentment is a lost ideology?

2. What things are holding you back from being content?
3. Should we be content with everything?

Day 24

Hebrews 12:1-2 Therefore, we also, since we are surrounded by so great a cloud of witnesses, let us lay aside every weight, and the sin which so easily ensnares us, and let us run with endurance the race that is set before us, (2) looking unto Jesus, the author and finisher of our faith, who for the joy that was set before Him endured the cross, despising the shame, and has sat down at the right hand of the throne of God.

    In the fourth lesson of this study, we looked at pressing on toward the goal. Philippians 3 is one of my favorite chapters in the bible. The chapter is very basic, but it has the ability to bring back into focus things we need to remember. These verses are some that drive me forward. It reminds me I am not alone, and I am not the first one to experience these things. We may be surprised at how many people deal with the same things we do. I can remember years ago a popular kid saying he did something I used to do. It connected me to him, for we had a shared experience.

    When others are going through the same things you are, it gives you strength to endure what you are facing. Endurance gives you a different kind of strength than momentary pressure. I go to the gym and I lift weights and I use an elliptical. Both types of exercise are different, but they are meant to accomplish two different things. I have heard people say endurance training is pointless. I strongly disagree. Endurance training gives you the ability to push harder and longer than you could have otherwise. These types of training are not separate, instead, they are tied together. Training for battle requires both momentary strengths to fight, and the enduring strength to march into battle. When you have someone cheering you on when you want to quit, it can make you dig deeper and find strength you did not even know you had.

Endurance causes you to grow beyond what you could normally do. Do not listen to the world when it says do not waste your time on things that do not benefit you. They have their opinions, but we have the results. Your faith will not grow unless you push yourself beyond your normal boundaries. You will not grow until you conclude you are not satisfied where you are. If others can do it, so can you. If they can push beyond their pains and make it, so can I.

I read about a marine who was running a marathon in honor of his fallen comrades. He got to the point he could no longer stand. He was completely out of energy and he hit the ground. The man went back to basic instincts in combat training and began to crawl. He finished the last leg of the race on his hands and knees. He did not quit, He would not quit because honoring his friends was more important than stopping.

Endurance is mustering up the strength to do what you said you would do. Work towards it, and do it. It is not easy, and it will take effort, but at the end you will be stronger and more able to handle the next challenge that lays before you.

1. What kinds of things motivate you to endure longer?
2. Who do you admire when you aspire to be more than what you are now? (Not just Jesus)
3. What things can you jettison out of your life that causes you to quit before you have met your goal?
4. How are you going to fix it?

Day 25

Matthew 5:9-12 Blessed are the peacemakers, for they shall be called sons of God. (10) Blessed are those who are persecuted for righteousness' sake, for theirs is the kingdom of heaven. (11) "Blessed are you when they revile and persecute you, and say all kinds of evil against you falsely for My sake. (12) Rejoice and be exceedingly glad, for great is your reward in heaven, for so they persecuted the prophets who were before you.

    As of late, I have become more of a Star Wars nerd. In the Sith code, there is a line that says, "Peace is a lie there is only passion." Although I do not agree with the second part of that phrase, I do believe peace outside of Christ is a lie. There are two different types of peace. Peace with God and peace with the world, and we can only have one of them. If you want peace with the world, you will have enmity towards God. However, if you want peace with God, you will not be able to be at peace with the world. These two concepts cannot coexist as much as we try to do it.

    You must make the choice of what you want more. Whatever choice you make will bring conflict from the other. If you try to have peace with both, you have conflict with everyone including yourself. Peace keeping is a lie. People believe, if I just keep quiet and leave it alone, then it will all work out. It never does. Not dealing with something does not make it magically resolve itself. Keeping the peace only creates more conflict. You are expected to stand down the next time it happens, if you do not stand up at the beginning. You are not at peace, instead you are in limbo.

Peace is a lie when it keeps you from growing. Peace is a lie when it keeps you apart from God and His word. Peace is a lie when it creates fear and stagnation. You are called to go into battle putting on the full armor of God. Paul tells us in Ephesians there is no peace while we are in this world. Peace is a lie to create apathy and contentment in the wrong areas. We are warriors and what do warriors do. We fight. This is a battle we cannot afford to lose. This is a battle that we must participate in.

You have been called into battle to stand on the truth of God's word. You cannot be silent. You cannot let the hands of those who wish us harm to grab hold of us. We must move ahead battle gear equipped. We are to know our orders and carry them out. The peace we have is knowing God has our backs when we are fighting for Him. You are God's people. Fight against our true enemy, the devil. He has a hold of so many people, and it is our job to help them to see the grip he has on them. The grip he may have on us. He wants nothing more than to see us fail. Church do not let Him win, instead fight!

1. Why do we fall for the lie that we are to peacekeepers?
2. If we are not peacekeepers, what are we supposed to be?

3. How can we better equip ourselves to prepared to fight the battles we need to fight?

Day 26

Leviticus 11:44-45 For I am the LORD your God. You shall therefore consecrate yourselves, and you shall be holy; for I am holy. Neither shall you defile yourselves with any creeping thing that creeps on the earth. (45) For I am the LORD who brings you up out of the land of Egypt, to be your God. You shall therefore be holy, for I am holy.

    Holiness is one of those Christianese words we like to throw around. We talk about it, we preach about it, we sing about it, but what does it really mean? It can mean a lot of different things to a lot of different people. Holiness in the Greek simple means to be set apart. The application means to set ourselves apart from the world. That is a very vague understanding, but one that most people understand in thought, but not in practice.

    Holiness means to cast off all the things that connect us to the world. We are to shed them like a bad garment, and if you are like me, you probably have plenty to shed. Holiness is not just a noun that we use. It is also verb that we live out. The reason this matters is simple. We can say we are holy, but to be holy you must look and be different. People all the time pretend to be Christians. I know several personally that play the part, but they do not act the part. Holiness is a choice you must make in order to separate the things of the world out of your life.

Recently, I have been convicted of some things I need get out of my life. They hold no value and they have been inhibiting me from pursuing holiness with God. I keep using the word, but I want to explain in more detail what it is. Holiness is not one thing. It is the umbrella of our pursuit with the Lord. Everything we do should be under it. If it is outside of the umbrella, then it is not holy. I would list things like sin, personal pursuits, excuses, White Castles, and Ice Cream in this category. Talk to my wife about the last two. Holiness is understanding that our actions, our words, our service, our hearts, and our minds should be centered on Jesus. If our actions do not align with Jesus, it is not holy and should be removed. If our language is not something that would honor our God, we need to change it. If our minds focus on things not in pursuance with God, we need to cleanse it.

Holiness is an everyday, every moment choice that we make. It is not a list of things we must do. Instead, it is a lifestyle of ways that we must live. It is not about what you doing as much as why you are doing it. Holiness is being different for the sake of having a relationship with Jesus. Liken it to a marriage. When you are married, you give up the single lifestyle and everything it contains. Your life should focus on your marriage and not things you used to do. If your mind wonders out of the marriage realm and into the single's realm, then you are pursing things that honor yourself and not your marriage. If you align yourself with God, you are making the same pledge to God as if you are married to Him. You are saying I will not pursue any other things outside of your relationship with God. If you do, you are doing things unholy, and you must recommit to the covenant you made. Therefore, holiness is pursuing God and honoring Him above all else. Keep your commitment, for God will certainly keep His.

1. What things in your life can you remove to make your pursuit of holiness better?
2. Why is pursuing holiness so important?
3. Can a person be holy and not treat his/her relationship like a marriage?
4. Do you think the misunderstanding of holiness is the reason most people do not have a better relationship with God and others?

Day 27

Psalms 139:14 I will praise You, for I am fearfully and wonderfully made; Marvelous are Your works, and that my soul knows very well.

A painter can turn a blank canvas into a masterpiece. He sees the potential of the canvas before the first stroke with the brush is made. At the beginning, it is completely white. However, in the mind of the painter, He can see the painting that lies within and begins to unleash it. He reveals the beauty that exist and brings it light. Like the canvas, God looks at our lives and proclaims us to be His masterpiece. David recognized this and proclaimed that He was fearfully and wonderfully made. When you look at your life, what do you see; a masterpiece in the making, or something else? God sees you differently than you often see yourself because he sees your potential, and not what you are right now. He sees what you can be and not where you have been. You are His and He wants to take all those things that you have been dealing with, all the missed opportunities, all the broken promises, and all the mistakes that are in your life removing them completely from you. He wants to remake you, remold you into something better. He sees you for what you are. You are a child of God. You are not worthless, and you are not unworthy. You are worth investing, and if you will let the Lord, He will turn your mess into a masterpiece. He will shape you and mold you into His prized pocession, no matter what you are now. If you allow Him to guide and direct you, you will be more than what you thought you ever could.

Therefore, let the Lord, who makes all things and sustains all things, make you into something grand. At the same time, never get into the mindset you are not good enough. Until this life is over, or until the Lord returns, God is working on you. He is remaking you, remolding you, He is directing you. Do not settle for what you think you are today. Instead, focus on what you can become. Let the Lord work, and let Him change you into something you never could have imagined. The painting at the beginning or in the middle may not look like much. But as the pieces all begin to fall into place, you begin to see the things you could not understand or envision before begin to take shape. As you see how God is directing you, do not strive to change things. He knows what He is doing let Him work, and you continue to be the masterpiece He wants you to be.

1. Why is it important to see yourself as a masterpiece in the making?
2. What things prevent people from seeing themselves this way?
3. What are some of the pitfalls of this type of thinking? How do we combat it?

Day 28

Proverbs 14:12 There is a way that seems right to a man, but its end is the way of death.

    One of the biggest lies we tell ourselves is we can do it ourselves. We do not need God, and we do not need anyone else to help. However, doing it ourselves only brings more pain than we can handle. Pain that destroys and pain that is unnecessary. Why do we convince ourselves that we can do something and we cannot? As I get older, my body reminds me of the fact I am not as young as I used to be. I started to weight lift again recently, and I am finding that my recovery is slower, and the pain tends to be more intense than I used to experience. It reminds me that If I do something more than I am capable, the pain is going to last much longer.

    People convince themselves all the time. I still got this, even when they are failing. They are drowning and the life preserver is right there beside them, but their pride is saying, "No, I do not need your help." The truth is we all need help. Help that comes from God and help that reminds us we are not in this alone. We do not have to keep on fighting the next battle without an army fighting with us. Men grew up believing a man does not ask for help and to do so indicates weakness. The source of true strength, however, is admitting that you cannot do something on your own. Physical strength is temporal and it is limited. True strength is being confident in yourself to know when you need help. Women are not immune to this either because the fear of failure and disappointing someone is constantly weighing on them. Both things are lies that people believe.

The truth is we all get sucked into the lies from time to time to the point we feel overwhelmed. Then we feel alone and trapped because we have gotten in too deep. That is when you take a deep breath and call for help. We must take on the attitude that help is a good thing. I watched hundreds of workers move an entire barn with just their bodies, no equipment was necessary. They were able to accomplish that amazing feat by everyone picking up the section of the barn they were assigned. You cannot pick up more than you are able, but when you have help, you can do things you never thought you could. The key to changing the way you live is changing the way you think. Help is not a weakness and doing it alone is not strength. It is only when you realize this truth that your life will forever be changed.

1. Why do you think people believe asking for help is a weakness?
2. Why has dependance become demonized in the eyes of so many?
3. What ways can we change how we view asking for help?
4.

Day 29

1John 1:9-10 If we confess our sins, He is faithful and just to forgive us our sins and to cleanse us from all unrighteousness. (10) If we say that we have not sinned, we make Him a liar, and His word is not in us.

Honesty is the key to experiencing reality correctly. When you have a perverted view of reality, it blinds you from the truth. For instance, what is happening in our country with men believing they are women and women believing they are men is a perversion of truth. People are blinded from reality because they do not like themselves and they want to be someone else. That does not change reality. It only changes your attitude towards it.

When we come to realize that we are sinners and in need of a savior, it changes our perspective. We convince ourselves we do not need Jesus. We do not need forgiveness. We pretend that God does not exist in order to have no accountability to anyone. We try to fight reality by convincing ourselves God just wants me to be happy. One of the biggest lies that we tell ourselves is something that we know is wrong, but we convince ourselves it will improve our lives.

We convince ourselves that yelling and screaming at someone is justified. I mean they messed up and deserved it, right? That one hurts me a lot because I am guilty of it. We convince ourselves that watching that R rated movie is okay because "we can handle it." "It's only one sex scene and it is not that bad." "That is just the ways things are today." "I know it is not good, but I can stop it anytime I want." "I do not need your help. I can do it on my own." We can fill this paragraph full of things we have done and excuses we have made. If I were to sit down and really think about it, I could fill a ten-page paper or more of all the excuses I have made all these years. I can understand why Isaiah says my righteousness is nothing more than filthy rags.

    It takes a lot of honesty to admit your life is broken. It takes a lot of guts to know you need God. It takes a lot of courage to say I know I have been living a false life, but I want to live differently from this day forward. I do not know where you are in your walk with Jesus. I know I am not where I need to be. If I know anything about people, I know you are not either. Here is the thing, that is okay. What is not okay is for us to believe that not being where we are supposed to be is an excuse for not striving for being better. God cares about the birds of the sky. He knows every hair on your head. He loves you and wants you to strive for more than what you thought possible. Do not give up on Him and more importantly do not give up on yourself. You are valuable and you are loved. Do not buy into the lie you are not.

1. Why do people convince themselves they are better than they are?
2. How do we change our hearts to better understand personal growth and the need for an honest heart?

3. In what ways can changing your heart and mind, change your reality?
4. What is the most important lesson you can take away from this?

Day 30

Revelation 2:5 Remember therefore from where you have fallen; repent and do the first works, or else I will come to you quickly and remove your lampstand from its place—unless you repent.

Let's bring it all together. In this devotional, we have talked about a lot of different things. But they all fall back to one theme: getting rid of all the stuff that clutters our lives and keeps us away from the Lord. This is an important work and a continual journey. It is not one easily traversed, but it is well worth the effort. As I have traveled along with this journey writing this, I had to take a lot of inventory of my personal life, and I have managed to root out some things causing issues in my life as well. My hope and prayer for you in this journey has been you have taken something from it as well and have grown. Remember who you serve and why you serve Him. Keep your focus on the Lord and do not let go of what is most important, your faith. Do not compromise because it is easy, and do not give in because it is convenient.

God has great things for you. You are His masterpiece and you are greatly loved. But make sure what you are offering him is your best and not the rest. Jettison anything out of your life you do not need in this journey. There is no reason to take along any excess cargo. It is not worth the price you pay for carrying around the things that have no value. It is time, if you have not already, to make yourself into the image God create you to be, not who you envision yourself to be. They are often not the same. I am living proof of this fact. However, do not get caught in the trap you will never be good enough. It is not your decision what you believe is good enough for God. If you are trying and you refuse to give up on your faith and on God, you are better off than you realize. The only time that you truly fail is when you decide to quit. If you talk to anyone who has been a Christian for any great amount of time, they will tell you the change in your life and in your relationships is not something you experience overnight. It is a life-long pursuit, and you are never done.

I want to leave you with this final thought. Our God is both the God of hills and the valleys. Our God is with us even when we do not feel like it. He is with us when we feel like we do not need Him, and He is with us when we think He is not there. He will not leave you nor forsake you. However, it depends on you to follow Him. Commit your life to Him and obey His word. He will guide you. He will change you. The key is to let Him, even if it hurts. Let it go and let it fall behind you. You do not need it anyway, because God does not get rid of the best. He gets rid of the junk.

1. What inventory have you taken along this journey?
2. What things have you been able to jettison from your life?

3. Why is it important to see yourself in God's eyes instead of your own?
4. What has been some of your biggest take aways from this devotional?